Engines of
INGENUITY

Engines of
INGENUITY

KIT WILLIAMS

ACKNOWLEDGEMENTS

✻

Angel Gould	The Overflier
Ged Lennox	The Bookmaker
Mike Rignall	The Helpful Engineer
Dorothy Marsden	The Model
Michael Goldfarb	The joyful
Mo Cohen	Who discovered Europe

✻

With a special thanks to my wife
Eleyne

© Kit Williams 2001
Published in 2001
Gingko Press
5768 Paradise Drive, Suite J
Corte Madera, CA 94925
Tel: 415 924 9615
Fax: 415 924 9608
email: books@gingkopress.com
ISBN: 1-58423-106-8

Produced by EPE Books, Highcroft, South Woodchester GL5 5EP
Printed in England by Colorworks, Chesterfield

ENGINES OF INGENUITY

THE BEGINNING

the South-Pointing Chariot

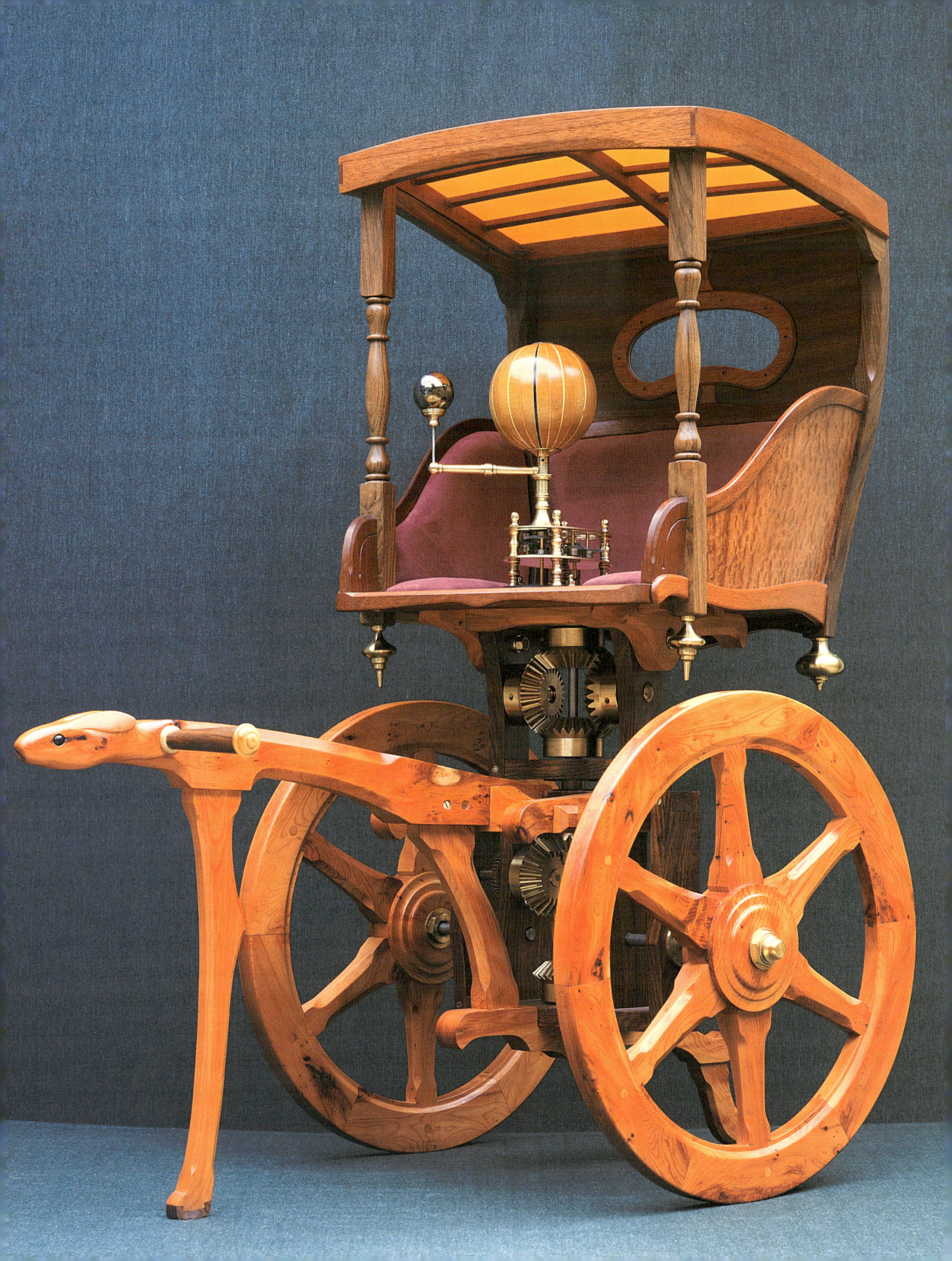

ENGINES OF INGENUITY

with wheels and gears

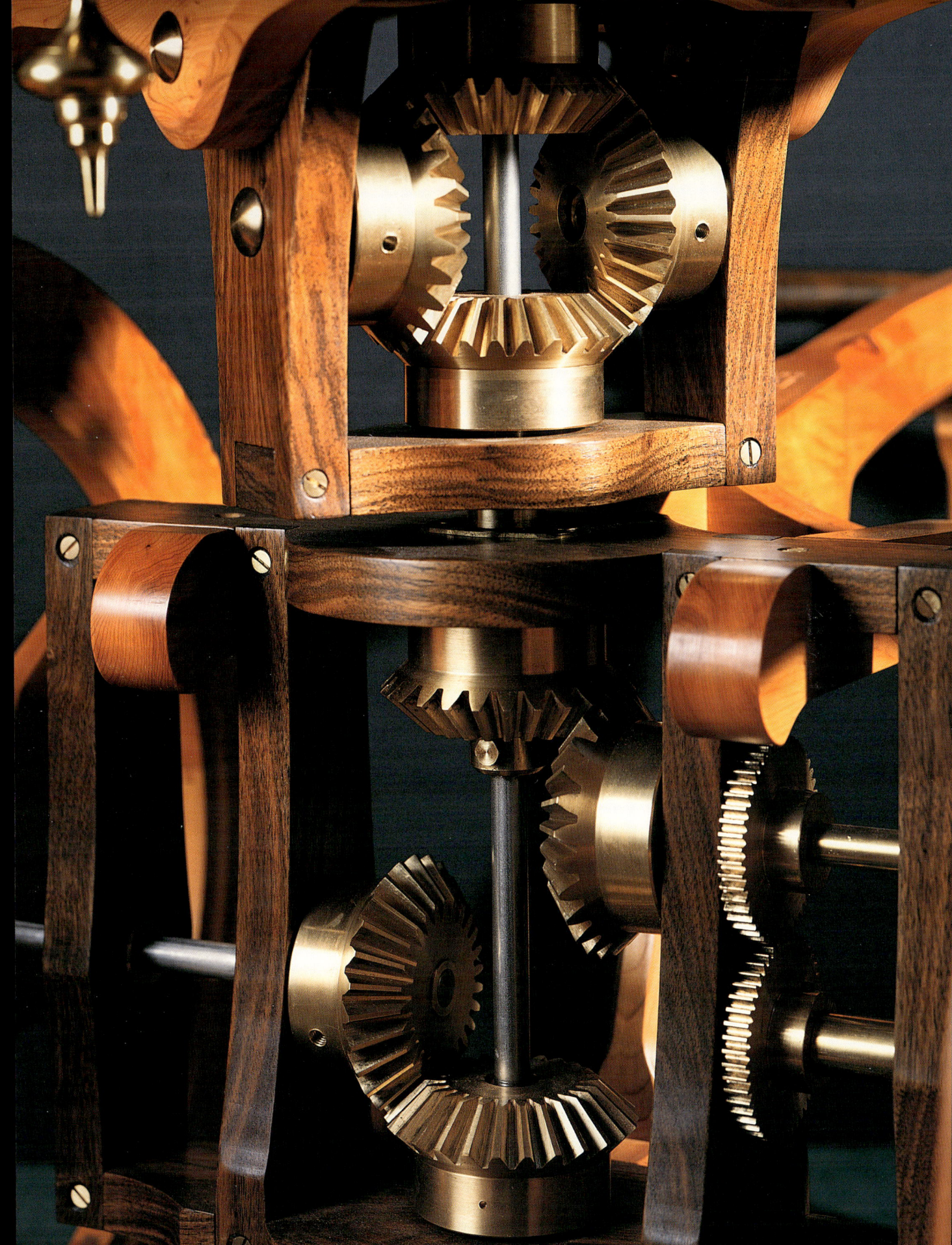

The Yellow Emperor

"*How will I* know?" said Huang Di, the Yellow Emperor, who knew everything, but wished to know more.

"How will I know the direction to take, by day and by night, in clear skies or cloudy, to arrive at a state of greater harmony? You see I am so often afraid."

"Let us call upon Fang Bo, your master craftsman, to help," said the Lady of the Black Peony. "As water conquers fire, your fears will be quenched."

So it was that in the third millennium BC the South-Pointing Chariot came into being; a machine equipped with wheels and gears that always ensured a south-facing aspect, no matter which way the chariot was pulled, pushed, or turned.

Huang Di journeyed in comfort, with the warmth of the sun shining always upon him.

ENGINES OF INGENUITY

II

ENGINES OF INGENUITY

journeyed in comfort,
with the warmth of the Sun

pawprints in the dust

Daedalus

"*Which way? Which* way next?" thought Daedalus as he dragged large wooden wheels behind him, calculating distances and marking the hot dusty ground with parallel lines; drawing a great picture in the sand; describing interlocking pathways, turning this way and that, but never crossing.

His brow glistened with the dew of his perspiration. His mind, full of Labrynthine Laws, ached. His thoughts were punctured by the angry screams of a large bird.

"Would that she cast her black mantle a little more between me and the Sun," thought Daedalus, looking skyward.

At that moment a small creature, a rabbit, scurried past him, pawprints in the dust, and disappeared down a hole. The solution was plain to see; not a construction of walls and galleries, but dark subterranean tunnels, conduits and stairways, ever entwining.

A place contrived
                to entangle
                              a man's sensibilities.

turning this way and that

ENGINES OF INGENUITY

ENGINES OF INGENUITY

Leonardo da Vinci

No Lady in a black dress came to Leonardo. He strictly forbade it.

Blood was on his hands and engines of war in his mind.

Before him on the table lay half-worked drawings, of a chariot, equipped with gears coupled to a platform that would always point towards the enemy, no matter which way the horses were driven. Sketched behind a little window, in a wooden shield, were the scrawled figures of archers with cross-bows.

But the gears wouldn't come together.

The ideas wouldn't mesh.

Differential impossibilities remained.

"My papers! I must arrange my papers! More light! Wax candles! I must have more light!"

In the unsettled panic of the night, the sound of red shoes could still be heard pacing back and forth in the street outside.

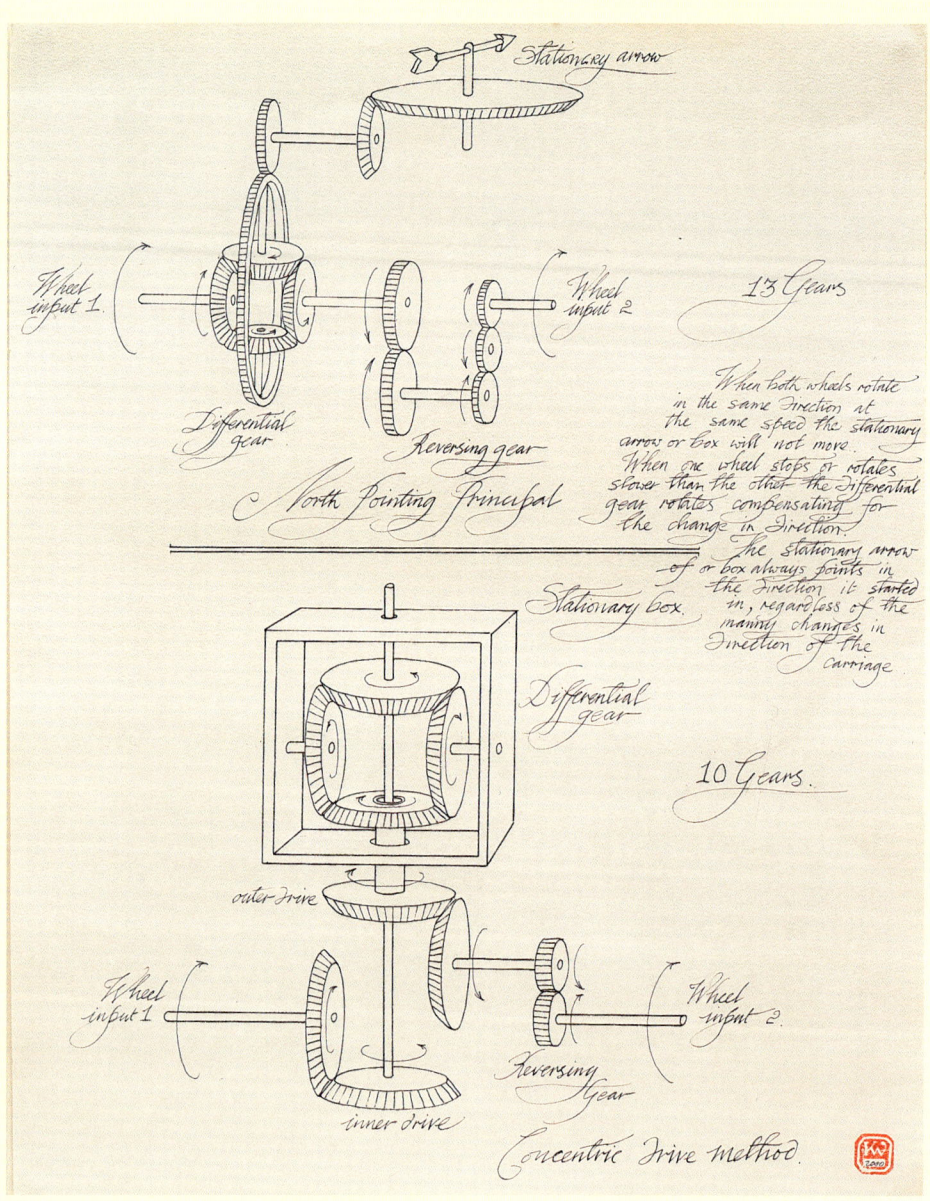

a little window
in a wooden shield

ENGINES OF INGENUITY

the clockmaker's universe

Sir Isaac Newton

Under the legs of the table a dog slept, dreaming of rabitting in hedge-bottoms. A moth entered the open window, attracted by a candle on the table. With singed wings, in panic it tumbled maddeningly about the room, waking the dog.

Out of the dream and into the chase, the dog leapt from floor to chair; from chair to table.

The candlestick upset.

Flame licked over liquid wax spilt on reams of paper. The smell of burning, and wisps of smoke, brought Isaac Newton running. Charred scraps, still in suspension floated to the floor.

"Diamond! Diamond!

Thou little knowest the mischief done!"

Who helped Newton re-assemble his papers? Who, in black dress with raven's quill, re-penned the *Principia Mathematica?* Who put together again the clockmaker's universe, put the Moon into its orbit, dictated the terms of Differential Calculus?

ENGINES OF INGENUITY

Jump now! It's your turn! Jump.

Soon you may see...

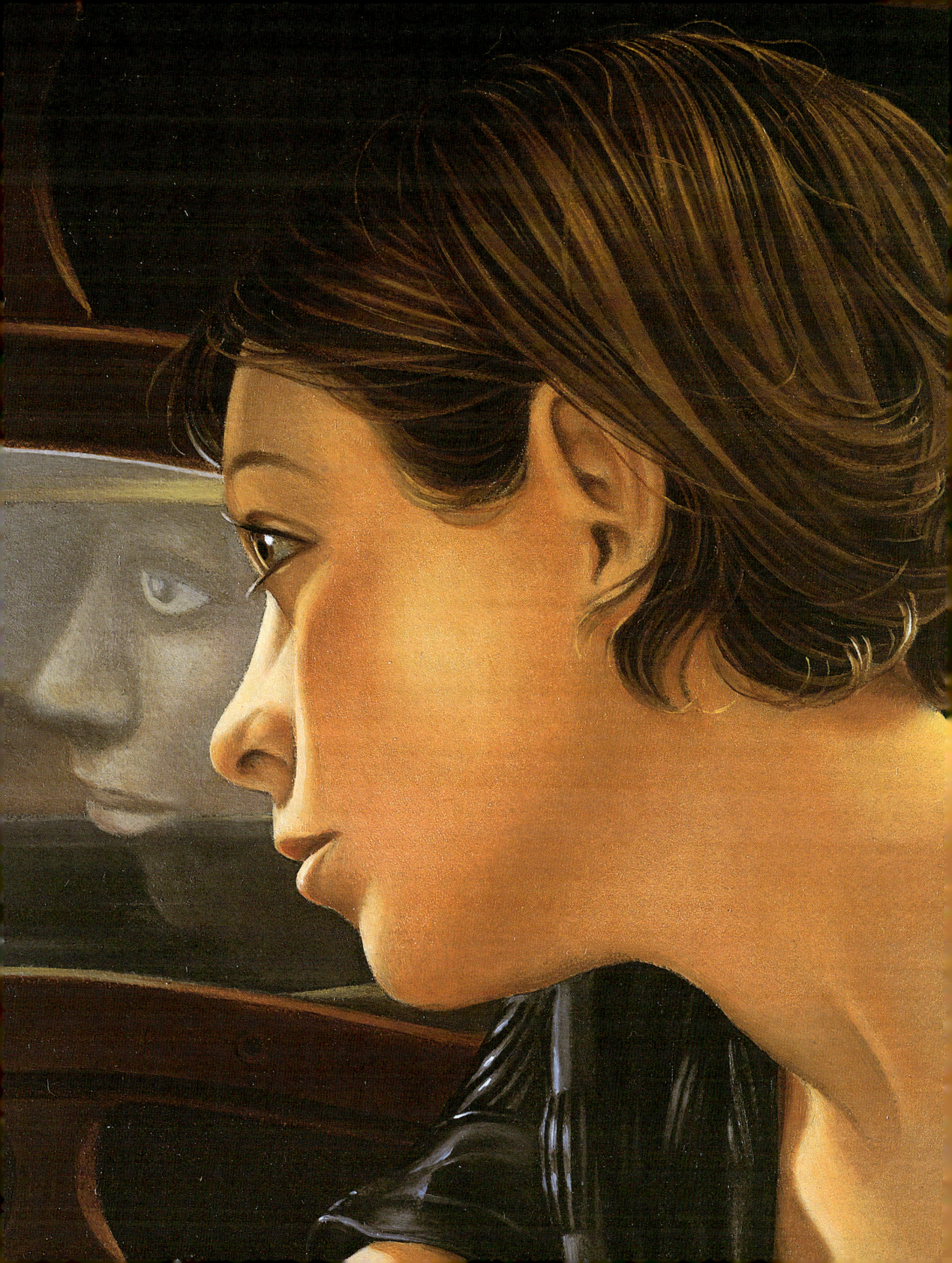

Elegy

Today I stand in singular audience, watching her travel alone; in carrion comfort; a side-show.

Jingle-jangle tunes play in the pit of creation, which once gave birth to the music of the spheres. Gears turn; ratchets click; time passes almost imperceptibly.

"Metaphysics! Quantum physics! Take your pick! See the Natural Laws turned upside down and stood upon their heads!"

Big ideas foundering on small intangibilities.

"Jump now! It's your turn! Jump through the hoop! No time to spare! Don't stay to watch the Sun go down!"

You didn't jump.
You tarried.
How wise!
Soon you may see what The Lady in Black sees.
Wait a while.
Stay...

THE END

ENGINES OF INGENUITY